EASY
SPANISH
DISHES

EASY
SPANISH
DISHES

SAFEWAY/GOOD HOUSEKEEPING

COOKERY NOTES

All spoon measures are level unless otherwise stated.

Size 2 eggs should be used except when otherwise stated.

Granulated sugar is used unless otherwise stated.

The oven should be preheated to the required temperature unless otherwise stated.

Text and illustrations copyright © Ebury Press and the National Magazine
Company Ltd 1994

Published exclusively for
Safeway
6 Millington Road, Hayes, Middlesex UB3 4AY
by Ebury Press
A division of Random House
20 Vauxhall Bridge Road
London SW1V 2SA

First published 1994

Edited by Julia Canning, Christine McFadden and Louise Steele
Recipes by Good Housekeeping Institute, Jacqueline Clarke
and Linda Frazer
Designed by Behram Kapadia
Photography by Michelle Garrett
Food stylist Liz Trigg

The paper in this book is acid-free

Typeset by Textype Typesetters, Cambridge
Printed in Italy

ISBN 0-09-182500-8

CONTENTS

Introduction *8*

Starters and Snacks *10*

Egg Dishes *24*

Poultry and Meat Dishes *32*

Fish and Shellfish Dishes *46*

Vegetable Dishes and Salads *54*

Sweet Treats *66*

FOREWORD

Welcome to *Easy Spanish Dishes*, part of the exciting new *Cooking Around the World* series produced in association with Safeway.

Each of the six books in this unique series is dedicated to one of the countries of the world most renowned for its mouthwatering cuisine. All the recipes have been double tested by the cooks in the Good Housekeeping Institute using Safeway's quality produce.

Presented in a clear, step-by-step format, many of the recipes are quick and easy enough to suit the hectic pace of modern living, although anyone looking to create an exotic feast for a really special occasion will not be disappointed.

To take the 'worry factor' out of using new ingredients, you will find tips on how to identify, select and prepare exotic fruit and vegetables, aromatic herbs and spices and other produce in the introductory pages.

Through the *Cooking Around the World* series you can bring the tastes and flavours of six fascinating countries to your table.

MOYRA FRASER
Cookery Editor
Good Housekeeping

INTRODUCTION

The food of Spain is very colourful and full of robust flavours. Sweet peppers, tomatoes, oranges and bright-yellow saffron give dishes vibrant colour, while an abundant use of garlic, olives, anchovies, almonds and chillies adds to the distinctive character of Spanish cooking. Classic dishes like Gazpacho – a delicious chilled vegetable soup – and Tortilla – a clever combination of egg and potato – are just two examples of Spanish cuisine, but there are many more exciting and flavour-rich dishes to explore.

TAPAS

The Spanish know how to enjoy food and are particularly fond of small snacks, known as tapas, which are consumed before lunch and dinner with a glass of wine, sherry or beer. Tapas bars serving these delicious snacks are found throughout Spain, even in the tiniest villages. The snacks can vary from simple slices of local cheese or chorizo sausage to more elaborate dishes of garlic prawns, salt cod balls or tiny meat pies. In fact, anything served in small quantities can be considered a tapas.

SPICES

As a result of ancient influences from the East, spices feature strongly in Spanish cooking.

SAFFRON Made from the stamens of the purple crocus flower, saffron is the most expensive spice in the world and gives the characteristic yellow colour and musty flavour to many Spanish rice dishes, notably paella. Saffron strands must be soaked in warm water or milk for about 10 minutes before using. Powdered saffron is also available and can be added straight to a dish by the pinch. Although inexpensive and convenient to use, powdered saffron is considered inferior to the saffron threads.

PAPRIKA Also known as 'pimenton', paprika is made from ground dried sweet red peppers. It is used to season many Spanish dishes and is an integral flavour of chorizo sausage. The flavour can vary from sweet to fiercely hot.

CINNAMON is the bark of a tree which grows in tropical forests. Sold in sticks or in ground form, it has a highly aromatic flavour and is popular for flavouring sweet dishes.

ALMONDS

Sweet almonds are used frequently in Spanish cooking in both savoury and sweet dishes, cakes and pastries. They are often toasted and salted to serve as tapas with a glass of dry sherry. In their ground form, they are traditionally used in savoury sauces, both as a thickening agent and as a flavouring. Ground almonds are also popular in sweet tarts and, mixed with honey, they make a delicious sweetmeat.

SEAFOOD

The extensive coastline of Spain lends itself to a plethora of seafood dishes. Many varieties of fish and shellfish are used – anchovies, tuna, prawns, sardines, mussels and squid, to mention a few.

SALT COD This Spanish delicacy, called 'bacalao' in Spain, is cod that has been salted and dried. It is an extremely popular ingredient in Spanish cooking. The flesh is firm, creamy-coloured and coated with a fine dusting of salt. Before using, salt cod must be soaked in cold water for at least 24 hours, changing the water frequently during this time, and draining it well before use.

ANCHOVIES These small sea fish are enjoyed in many ways – as pizza toppings, in flans, sauces, salads and salad dressings. Anchovies are mainly only available fresh in the Mediterranean regions where they are caught. For export they are more often filleted and preserved in brine or oil and packed in small flat cans. To reduce the saltiness of anchovies, drain them from the liquid in which they are packed and soak in milk for up to 20 minutes, then drain again and pat dry before using as required.

SARDINES These silver-skinned, oily fish measure between 10-20 cm (4-8 in) in length and are delicious grilled. Fresh sardines are now available throughout the year.

CHORIZO SAUSAGE

Chorizo is the most common smoked Spanish sausage and finds its way into many Spanish dishes. Made from pork meat and fat, chorizo is heavily flavoured with garlic as well as paprika. It can be eaten both raw and cooked and is exceptionally good grilled over charcoal.

RICE

Of all the colourful rice dishes made, classic paella which includes both seafood and chicken, is undoubtedly the best known. However, there are many different versions which are just as interesting and delicious. Paellas are usually made with short-grained rice.

VEGETABLES AND PULSES

Certain vegetables are particularly associated with Spanish cooking.

ONIONS Spanish onions are large, mild and juicy. They are renowned for their sweet flavour and are one of the best types of onion to use raw in salads.

GARLIC Fresh garlic is a favourite seasoning for many Spanish dishes, a classic example being garlic-flavoured prawns. When buying garlic, select bulbs that are firm and hard – the less papery the skin the more moist and fresh the cloves will be.

PIMIENTOS are synonymous with Spanish foods. Literally translated, pimiento means pepper, but the name is generally applied to red peppers. To prepare pimientos at home Spanish-style, simply roast sweet red peppers in a moderate oven for just over 30 minutes, turning from time to time, then remove the skin and seeds and store the flesh in a covered container in the refrigerator for up to 4 days. The Spanish are also fond of dried sweet red peppers which are commonly used to flavour salt cod.

OLIVES Like many other Mediterranean countries, Spain produces a large amount of olives and olive oil. The oil is used widely for cooking and as a dressing for salad or boiled potatoes. The olives – black or green – are marinated in brine and served as yet another tapas, perhaps stuffed with anchovy or pimiento.

CHICK-PEAS Called 'garbanzo' in Spanish, chick-peas are an essential ingredient for many of the robust country dishes. These heart-shaped, beige coloured peas are available dried or canned.

SHERRY

Sherry is the most famous drink to come from Spain. A popular aperitif, it can be also drunk as a dessert wine. Sherry is available in different degrees of sweetness ranging from the extra dry finos to the medium wines such as amontillado, to the rich sweetness of the cream sherries at the other end of the scale. Sherry also plays an important role in Spanish cooking and makes a splendid addition to both savoury and sweet dishes.

STARTERS AND
SNACKS

The delicious savouries given in this chapter make a palate-tingling start to a meal or, for an authentic touch, try offering them with a glass of dry sherry as a tapas – the Spanish term for a snack served before a main meal. Choose from classic Spanish delicacies such as prawns dipped in garlic sauce, tasty little balls of salt cod, refreshing spiced carrots and bite-sized meat turnovers to bring the colourful atmosphere of a tapas bar into your home.

OPPOSITE
TOP Fish and Leek Soup
BOTTOM Spicy Meat Turnovers

FISH AND LEEK SOUP

SERVES 6

2 × 15 ml tbs olive oil

335 g (12 oz) leeks, halved lengthways and sliced

225 g (8 oz) potatoes, diced

2 garlic cloves, skinned and crushed

900 ml (1½ pt) water

225 g (8 oz) cod fillets, skinned and cut into bite-size cubes

salt and pepper

1 Heat the oil in a large saucepan and cook the leeks over a moderate heat for 5-8 minutes until softened. Add the potatoes and garlic and cook for 2-3 minutes.

2 Stir in the water and bring to the boil. Reduce the heat, cover the pan and simmer for 25 minutes until the potatoes are tender.

3 Add the cod cubes and continue cooking for about 3-5 minutes or until the fish is tender and cooked. Season to taste with salt and pepper and serve hot.

COOK'S TIP

For an attractive look to the soup, choose leeks which have plenty of green parts.

This soup can also be made with salt cod – soak the salt cod for 24 hours, changing the water frequently, before using. Add the drained salt cod to the pan in step 2 and cook for 25 minutes until tender.

GAZPACHO

SERVES 6

2 thick slices white bread, crusts removed

2 garlic cloves, skinned and halved

4 × 15 ml tbs olive oil

400 g can chopped tomatoes

565 g (1¼ lb) ripe tomatoes, roughly chopped

½ cucumber

1 red pepper, seeded

6 salad onions, trimmed

1 × 15 ml tbs red wine vinegar

2 × 5 ml tsp chopped fresh tarragon

salt and pepper

150 ml (5 fl oz) olive oil, for frying

tarragon ice cubes, to garnish

1 Tear up one of the slices of bread and put in a food processor or blender. Add the garlic cloves. With the motor running, slowly add the olive oil, until the mixture is smooth. Add the canned and fresh tomatoes.

2 Cut a quarter each of the cucumber and pepper into dice and slice one salad onion. Reserve. Roughly chop the remaining vegetables and add to the tomatoes. Blend until almost smooth.

3 Add the vinegar and tarragon then season to taste with salt and pepper. Transfer to a bowl, cover and chill.

4 Slice the remaining bread into small squares. Heat the olive oil in a pan and fry the bread until golden. Drain on absorbent kitchen paper.

5 Serve the chilled gazpacho with the reserved vegetables and croûtons just before serving and garnish with tarragon ice cubes.

COOK'S TIP

To make tarragon ice cubes, place fresh tarragon leaves in ice cube trays, top up with water and freeze until solid.

Gazpacho

SPANISH PRAWN FRITTERS

SERVES 4-6

3 × 15 ml tbs olive oil
50 g (2 oz) finely chopped onion
1 × 5 ml tsp paprika
3 × 15 ml tbs chopped fresh parsley
50 g (2 oz) plain flour
½ × 5 ml tsp baking powder
3 × 15 ml tbs water
salt and pepper
115 g (4 oz) cooked, peeled prawns, finely chopped
vegetable oil, for frying

1 Heat the olive oil in a small saucepan. Add the onion and gently fry, covered, until soft. Add paprika and parsley and cook for 1 minute, stirring. Allow to cool.

2 In a bowl, mix the flour and baking powder with the water and seasoning. Stir in the prawns and the onion mixture.

3 Heat about 0.6 cm (¼ in) vegetable oil in a frying pan. Add 15 ml tbs mounds of the mixture to the pan and fry until golden. Drain and serve hot.

SALT COD BALLS

SERVES 4-6

225 g (8 oz) dried salt cod
675 g (1½ lb) floury potatoes
1 garlic clove, skinned and crushed
3 × 15 ml tbs chopped fresh parsley
1 egg yolk, beaten
pepper
vegetable oil, for frying
sprigs of flat-leaf parsley, to garnish
lemon wedges, to serve

1 Soak the cod in cold water for 24 hours, changing the water four times. Drain the cod and break up finely removing any skin or bones.

2 Boil the potatoes until tender. Drain and mash with the garlic, parsley and egg yolk. Add the cod and season with pepper.

3 With lightly floured hands, shape the mixture into about 20 walnut-sized balls. Heat the oil in a deep-fat fryer to 180°C/350°F or until a cube of stale bread turns brown in 40 seconds. Fry in batches until golden brown. Drain on absorbent kitchen paper. Garnish with parsley sprigs and serve with wedges of lemon.

PRAWNS WITH GARLIC AND OIL

SERVES 4

about 900 g (2 lb) cooked shell on prawns
2-5 large juicy garlic cloves, skinned
40 g (1½ oz) ground almonds
salt
5 × 15 ml tbs chopped fresh parsley
1 × 5 ml tsp paprika
about 300 ml (10 fl oz) extra-virgin olive oil
juice of ½ lemon
lemon slices and flat-leaf parsley, to garnish

1 Peel the prawns, arrange on a serving platter and chill.

2 To make the sauce, put the garlic, ground almonds, salt to taste, parsley and paprika in a blender or food processor and blend for about 1 minute. With the motor running, carefully add the oil, in a thin stream.

3 When all the oil has been incorporated, gradually pour in the lemon juice and blend for 30 seconds until thick. Serve with the prawns as a dip. Garnish prawns with lemon and parsley.

TOP Prawns with Garlic and Oil
BOTTOM Salt Cod Balls

GRILLED SARDINES WITH FRESH TOMATO SAUCE

SERVES 4

16 small or 8 large sardines, cleaned

2 × 15 ml tbs olive oil

few sprigs of fresh thyme

pepper

juice of ½ lemon

lemon rind shreds, to garnish

TOMATO SAUCE

1 × 15 ml tbs olive oil

1 small onion, skinned and finely chopped

1 garlic clove, skinned and finely chopped

450 g (1 lb) ripe tomatoes, finely chopped

1 × 15 ml tbs fresh chopped parsley

salt and pepper

1 To make the tomato sauce, heat the oil in a pan, add the onion and garlic and fry gently until the onion is softened. Add the tomatoes and parsley, then season with salt and pepper to taste. Cook, uncovered, for 10-15 minutes until the tomatoes are just tender.

2 Meanwhile, score the fish with three or four diagonal cuts on each side. Brush with oil, and push a few sprigs of thyme into some of the cuts. Season with pepper and sprinkle with lemon juice.

3 Arrange the fish on grill rack and grill for about 4 minutes on each side or until cooked, brushing with the oil and juices frequently.

4 Arrange the cooked sardines on a platter, and pour over any juices from the grill pan. Garnish with lemon rind shreds, and serve with the tomato sauce.

Grilled Sardines with Fresh Tomato Sauce

KIDNEY AND CHICKEN KEBABS

SERVES 4

8 small lambs' kidneys, skinned, halved and cored

6 lean bacon rashers, quartered

2 boneless chicken breasts (preferably corn-fed), cut into 16 chunks

4 × 15 ml tbs olive oil

2 × 15 ml tbs sherry vinegar

1 garlic clove, skinned and crushed

salt and pepper

few sprigs of fresh thyme

2 × 15 ml tbs chopped fresh parsley

1 Soak 8 small wooden skewers in cold water for 30 minutes, then thread the kidney halves, pieces of bacon and chunks of chicken onto each skewer, alternating the ingredients. Place the kebabs in a shallow dish.

2 Whisk together the olive oil, vinegar and garlic with salt and pepper to taste. Pour over the kebabs. Tuck in the thyme sprigs and scatter half of the parsley over. Leave the kebabs to marinate for 20 minutes at room temperature or in the refrigerator for 2 hours, turning once or twice.

3 Lift the kebabs out of the marinade, allowing the marinade to drain back into the dish. Pat the kebabs dry with absorbent kitchen paper.

4 Arrange on a grill rack and grill for about 10 minutes, turning frequently and basting occasionally with the marinade. Scatter with the remaining parsley and serve hot with the cooking juices drizzled over the top.

COOK'S TIP

These kebabs are also suitable for barbecuing. Baste with the marinade during cooking.

Kidney and Chicken Kebabs

SPICY MEAT TURNOVERS

SERVES 6

PASTRY

175 ml (6 fl oz) water
1 × 5 ml tsp salt
50 g (2 oz) butter
2 × 15 ml tbs olive oil
300 g (11 oz) plain flour
2 egg yolks

FILLING

1 streaky bacon rasher, rinded and chopped
1 small onion, skinned and chopped
1 garlic clove, skinned and crushed
175 g (6 oz) lean minced beef, lamb or veal
2 × 5 ml tsp tomato purée
1 hot chilli, seeded and finely chopped (optional)
75 ml (3 fl oz) dry red wine
salt and pepper
1 × 15 ml tbs chopped fresh parsley
beaten egg, for brushing
vegetable oil, for frying

1 To make the pastry, heat the water with the salt, butter and oil until the butter has melted and the water is just boiling. Remove from heat, then quickly add the flour all at once. Beat vigorously with a wooden spoon then beat in the egg yolks.

2 Turn the dough on to a lightly floured surface and knead until smooth and elastic. Cover with a damp tea-towel and leave in a warm place for 20-30 minutes to rest.

3 To make the filling, gently fry the bacon in a heavy-based saucepan until the fat starts to run. Add the onion and garlic and fry over a high heat for 2 minutes. Add the meat and fry, stirring all the time until the meat is thoroughly browned. Add the tomato purée and chilli, if using and fry for 1 minute.

4 Stir in the wine, bring to the boil then cover and simmer gently for 30 minutes, stirring occasionally. Add a little water, if the mixture starts to stick. Season generously with salt and pepper, then stir in the parsley – the mixture should be thick but moist.

5 Roll out the pastry on a lightly floured surface and cut out 8 cm (3 in) rounds using a plain cutter. Place 1 × 5 ml tsp mixture on to each circle of pastry. Brush the edges with beaten egg. Fold in half then twist the edges together to seal.

6 Heat the oil in a deep-fat fryer to 190°C/375°F or until a cube of stale bread turns brown in 30 seconds. Fry the turnovers in batches for 2-3 minutes until golden brown. Drain on absorbent kitchen paper while frying the remainder. Keep warm in a low oven until ready to serve, or serve cold.

PORK AND HAM FLAMENQUINES

MAKES ABOUT 28

50 g (2 oz) butter
4 × 15 ml tbs plain flour
300 ml (10 fl oz) vegetable stock
salt and pepper
335 g (12 oz) pork fillet
150 g (5 oz) thinly sliced cured ham
115 g (4 oz) dried white breadcrumbs
4 garlic cloves, skinned and crushed
4 × 15 ml tbs chopped fresh parsley
2 eggs, beaten
vegetable oil, for frying

1 Melt the butter in a saucepan and add the flour. Gently fry for 1 minute, stirring, then gradually add the stock. Bring to the boil and cook, stirring constantly, until thickened. Pour the sauce into a bowl, season to taste with salt and pepper and cool.

2 Thinly slice the pork fillet and roll a piece of ham around each slice. Spread the sauce over the

Pork and Ham Flamenquines

rolls and place on baking trays lined with non-stick baking parchment. Chill for at least 2 hours.

3 Combine the breadcrumbs, garlic and parsley. Coat the rolls in beaten egg and then in the breadcrumb mixture. Chill for 30 minutes.

4 Heat the oil in a deep-fat fryer to 180°C/350°F or until a cube of stale bread turns brown in 40 seconds. Fry in batches for 2-3 minutes until well browned. Drain on absorbent kitchen paper and keep warm, uncovered, in a low oven while frying the remainder. Serve hot.

ONION AND ANCHOVY PIZZA

SERVES 6-8

450 g (1 lb) strong white flour
½ × 5 ml tsp salt
1 sachet fast-action dried yeast
8 × 15 ml tbs olive oil
75 ml (3 fl oz) each of water and milk mixed together, warmed
2 large onions, skinned and thinly sliced
50 g can anchovy fillets, drained and roughly chopped
2 × 15 ml tbs pine kernels
2 × 15 ml tbs sultanas
1 × 5 ml tsp crushed dried chilli
pepper

1 Sift the flour and salt together into a large bowl. Stir in the yeast. Make a well in the centre and add 4 × 15 ml tbs olive oil with a little of the milk and water. Draw the flour and liquid together, gradually adding the remaining milk and water, until a dough is formed. Knead for about 10 minutes on a floured surface. Return to the bowl, cover with a cloth and leave in a warm place to rise for about 1 hour.

2 Heat the remaining olive oil in a large frying pan and gently fry the onions until just soft.

3 Knead the dough to knock out the air and roll out to a 30 × 38 cm/12 × 15 in rectangle. Place on an oiled baking tray. Cover with onions. Scatter the anchovies over the onions, along with the pine kernels, sultanas and chilli. Season with pepper.

4 Bake at 230°C/450°F/Gas Mark 8 for 10-12 minutes until the edges are beginning to brown. Cut into slices and serve warm.

SPICED CARROTS

SERVES 6

900 g (2 lb) carrots, cut into 0.6 cm (¼ in) diagonal slices
salt and pepper
115 ml (4 fl oz) olive oil
3 × 15 ml tbs red wine vinegar
2-3 garlic cloves, skinned and thinly sliced
2 small red chillies, seeded and finely chopped
2 × 15 ml tbs chopped fresh oregano or marjoram or 1 × 5 ml tsp dried
½ × 5 ml tsp ground cumin
1 × 5 ml tsp ground coriander

1 Cook the carrots in boiling, salted water until tender but still crunchy, then drain.

2 Whisk together the oil, vinegar, garlic, chillies, herbs, spices, and seasoning. Mix in the warm carrots and leave to cool.

3 When cold, cover and marinate in the refrigerator for at least 3 hours, stirring occasionally.

4 Leave to stand at room temperature for at least 30 minutes before serving.

COOK'S TIP

Chillies contain a pungent oil which can cause an unpleasant burning sensation to eyes and skin, so it is best to wear rubber gloves when preparing chillies and to be sure not to touch your face or eyes during preparation.

Onion and Anchovy Pizza

MUSHROOM TARTLETS

MAKES 24

PASTRY
225 g (8 oz) plain flour
large pinch of salt
115 g (4 oz) butter or margarine, cut into small pieces
3-4 × 15 ml tbs chilled water
FILLING
275 g (10 oz) mushrooms, wiped and chopped
1 garlic clove, skinned and crushed
8 × 15 ml tbs mayonnaise
4 × 15 ml tbs chopped fresh parsley
lemon juice, to taste
salt and pepper
strips of canned pimientos, sliced mushrooms and flat-leaf parsley, to garnish

1 To make the pastry, put the flour and salt in a bowl. Rub in the fat until the mixture resembles fine breadcrumbs. Sprinkle the water over the mixture and mix to make a stiff dough. Roll out on a lightly floured surface and cut out 7 cm (2¾ in) rounds using a fluted cutter. Place the rounds in 24 greased bun tins and prick the bases well with a fork.

2 Bake at 200°C/400°F/Gas Mark 6 for about 10-12 minutes or until slightly browned around the edges. Leave to cool in the tins for 2 minutes, then remove from the tins and cool on a wire rack.

3 About 1 hour before serving, mix the mushrooms with the garlic, mayonnaise, parsley, lemon juice and salt and pepper to taste. Pile into the tartlet cases. Garnish the tartlets with strips of pimiento, sliced mushrooms and flat-leaf parsley.

WRINKLED POTATOES WITH GARLIC AND PAPRIKA SAUCE

SERVES 4-6

2 × 15 ml tbs olive oil
675 g (1½ lb) small unpeeled new potatoes
1 × 5 ml tsp coarse salt
SAUCE
1 × 5 ml tsp cumin seeds
½ × 5 ml tsp salt
2 × 15 ml tbs white wine vinegar
1 × 5 ml tsp paprika
2 garlic cloves, skinned and crushed
115 ml (4 fl oz) olive oil
pepper

1 To make the sauce, put the cumin seeds, salt, vinegar, paprika and garlic in a processor or blender and blend until smooth. With the motor running, slowly add the oil in a thin stream until the mixture thickens. Season to taste with the pepper.

2 Heat the oil in a heavy-based pan large enough to hold the potatoes in one layer. Add the potatoes then reduce the heat to a minimum. Cover and cook for up to 30 minutes, shaking the pan occasionally, until the potatoes are tender and the skins are golden and wrinkled. Sprinkle with the salt.

3 Serve the potatoes with the sauce for dipping. Alternatively, serve the potatoes in small bowls with the sauce poured over.

TOP Wrinkled Potatoes with Garlic and Paprika Sauce
BOTTOM Mushroom Tartlets

EGG DISHES

Eggs are widely used in everyday Spanish cooking to produce an exciting range of nourishing lunch and supper dishes. The Spanish omelette, tortilla, is a well-known example. A delicious combination of egg, potato and onion, tortilla is a versatile dish which is even good served cold as part of a picnic spread. Other Spanish-style dishes to try include hard-boiled eggs stuffed with tuna, or eggs baked with a colourful mixture of peppers, tomatoes and ham — tasty food for all the family to enjoy.

OPPOSITE
Spanish Tortilla

SPANISH TORTILLA

SERVES 4

4 × 15 ml tbs olive oil

450g (1 lb) waxy potatoes (such as Maris Bard or Wilja), peeled and diced

2 onions, skinned and sliced

6 eggs

salt and pepper

1 Heat half the oil in a heavy-based, non-stick frying pan. Add the potatoes and onions and cook over a high heat for 1-2 minutes, stirring all the time, so that the potatoes are coated with oil and sealed on all sides.

2 Reduce the heat and cook for 5-10 minutes or until the potatoes are soft. Loosen any sediment at the bottom of the pan with a wooden spatula. Add a little extra oil, if necessary, and heat for 1 minute until very hot. Beat the eggs with a fork and season to taste with salt and pepper. Stir into the hot oil and potatoes.

3 Cook over a high heat for 1-2 minutes, then reduce the heat and cook until the eggs are just set. Loosen the tortilla from the sides of the pan, then turn it out on to a serving plate.

4 Heat the remaining oil in the pan, then add the tortilla, browned side up, and cook for a further 1-2 minutes. Serve warm or cold, cut in wedges.

COOK'S TIP

A Spanish omelette, or tortilla, should be much thicker than an ordinary omelette. Use a good heavy-based non-stick frying pan about 25 cm (10 in) in diameter to get the right depth with this number of eggs.

EGGS FLAMENCO

SERVES 4

2 × 15 ml tbs olive oil

½ large onion, skinned and finely chopped

227 g can chopped tomatoes

¼ × 5 ml tsp paprika

salt and pepper

8 asparagus spears

50 g (2 oz) frozen petits pois

75 g (3 oz) chorizo sausage, thinly sliced

1 canned pimiento, sliced

4 eggs

1 × 15 ml tbs chopped fresh parsley

1 Heat the olive oil in a saucepan, add the onion and gently fry until softened. Add the chopped tomatoes and paprika and season to taste with salt and pepper. Simmer, covered, for 10 minutes.

2 Cut the asparagus into 4 cm (1½ in) pieces. Cook in boiling, salted water for 2 minutes then add the peas and boil for a further 3 minutes. Drain.

3 Spoon the tomato sauce into the bottom of four individual shallow gratin dishes. Arrange the asparagus, peas, chorizo and pimiento around the edge of each dish then break an egg into the centre. Season to taste with salt and pepper and sprinkle with parsley.

4 Bake at 230°C/450°F/Gas Mark 8 for about 12 minutes until the eggs are set. Serve hot.

COOK'S TIP

For convenience for a family supper, cook the Eggs Flamenco in one large, shallow gratin dish instead of four individual dishes.

Eggs Flamenco

SPINACH PANCAKES

SERVES 6

PANCAKES

1 egg
150 ml (5 fl oz) milk
150 ml (5 fl oz) water
115 g (4 oz) plain flour
salt
15 g (½ oz) butter
spinach leaves, to garnish

FILLING

450 g (1 lb) fresh spinach
2 × 15 ml tbs olive oil
½ large onion, skinned and finely chopped
2 garlic cloves, skinned and crushed
1 × 5 ml tsp anchovy paste
salt and pepper
15 g (½ oz) freshly grated Parmesan cheese

1 To make the pancake batter, whisk together the egg, milk and water. Sift the flour and a pinch of salt into a bowl and make a well in the centre. Pour in the egg mixture, and gradually whisk in the flour, beating until smooth.

2 Melt a little butter in a 10-13 cm (4-5 in) diameter frying pan and pour in just enough batter to coat the pan. When the mixture has set, turn the pancake over and cook for a few more seconds. Remove the pancake from the pan. Repeat the process with the remaining batter, layering the pancakes between greaseproof paper. The batter should yield about twelve pancakes.

3 Wash the spinach, removing any tough stalks and put into a large saucepan without adding any extra water. Cover and cook over a high heat, shaking the pan from time to time, until the spinach has wilted. Squeeze out any excess moisture and chop roughly.

4 Heat the olive oil in a frying pan and add the onion. Gently fry until softened then add the garlic and gently fry for a further minute. Stir in the anchovy paste. Add the chopped spinach and mix well. Season to taste with salt and pepper, bearing in mind that the anchovy paste is quite salty.

5 Place a spoonful of the spinach mixture in the middle of each pancake and fold the edges over to form a square parcel. Place the filled pancakes in a baking dish and sprinkle each one with Parmesan cheese. Bake at 190°C/375°F/Gas Mark 5 for 10 minutes. Serve warm, garnished with spinach leaves.

MUSHROOM REVUELTO

SERVES 4

25 g (1 oz) butter
2 × 15 ml tbs olive oil
1 large garlic clove, skinned and crushed
450 g (1 lb) mixed mushrooms, sliced
¼ red pepper, seeded and finely diced
6 eggs, beaten
3 × 15 ml tbs milk
2 × 15 ml tbs chopped fresh parsley (optional)
½ dried red chilli, finely chopped
salt and pepper

1 Heat the butter and oil in a shallow pan, add the garlic, mushrooms and pepper and cook over moderate heat for 3-5 minutes until softened.

2 Beat together the eggs, milk, parsley and dried chilli and season to taste with salt and pepper. Pour into the pan and cook, stirring gently, until the eggs are set. Serve at once.

TOP Spinach Pancakes
BOTTOM Mushroom Revuelto

TUNA STUFFED EGGS

6 hard-boiled eggs
200 g can tuna fish in oil
1 × 15 ml tbs capers, drained
25 g (1 oz) pitted green olives, chopped
¼ × 5 ml tsp paprika
2 × 5 ml tsp chopped fresh parsley
3 × 15 ml tbs mayonnaise
salt and pepper
extra paprika, to garnish

1 Cut the hard-boiled eggs in half lengthways. Remove the yolks and set aside the whites. Press the yolks through a sieve into a bowl.
2 Drain the tuna and flake quite finely. Reserve 1 × 15 ml tbs of the sieved egg yolk and add the rest to the tuna.
3 Roughly chop the capers and add to the tuna, together with the olives, paprika, parsley and mayonnaise. Season to taste with salt and pepper.
4 Spoon the mixture into the egg whites, forming it into a dome shape, which almost covers the surface of the egg. Sprinkle each one with a little of the reserved egg yolk and garnish with a dusting of paprika.

COOK'S TIP

Serve these eggs on a bed of mixed green salad leaves tossed in a good vinaigrette, or with sliced large tomatoes, drizzled with garlic dressing to taste.

BAKED HAM TORTILLA

3 × 15 ml tbs olive oil
1 onion, skinned and chopped
2 garlic cloves, skinned and crushed
225 g (8 oz) gammon, diced
335 g (12 oz) tomatoes, skinned, seeded and diced
225 g (8 oz) green beans, cut into 2.5 cm (1 in) lengths
6 eggs
salt and pepper

1 Heat the oil in a saucepan, add the onion and cook over a moderate heat for 5 minutes until softened. Add the garlic and gammon and cook for 4-5 minutes, stirring frequently until beginning to brown.
2 Add the tomatoes and cook gently until softened, then stir in the beans and simmer for about 3 minutes until just tender. Transfer the mixture to a buttered, shallow baking dish.
3 Break the eggs into a bowl, season to taste with salt and pepper, then beat two or three times with a fork, just to break up the yolks and mix very lightly.
4 Pour the egg mixture into the baking dish and bake in the oven at 200°C/400°F/Gas Mark 6 for 15-20 minutes until set. Serve at once.

Baked Ham Tortilla

POULTRY AND
MEAT DISHES

Chicken casseroles and stews, robustly flavoured with garlic
and a variety of spices or herbs, are a typical feature of
Spanish cooking. Here you will find a good selection to
sample, from a classic combination of rice, chicken and
chorizo sausage to an aromatic dish flavoured with saffron
and almonds. Duckling cooked with green olives, roast pork
stuffed with figs and the traditional partnership of kidneys
and sherry are just a few more tasty ideas brought to you from
the Spanish kitchen.

FIESTA CHICKEN

SERVES 4

4 × 15 ml tbs olive oil

1 onion, skinned and chopped

2 garlic cloves, skinned and crushed

4 chicken portions

4 × 15 ml tbs brandy

1 small red and 1 small yellow pepper, seeded and sliced

4 large tomatoes, skinned and chopped

150 ml (5 fl oz) dry white wine

150 ml (5 fl oz) chicken stock or water

2 × 5 ml tsp chopped fresh rosemary or
1 × 5 ml tsp dried

salt and pepper

sprigs of rosemary, to garnish

1 Heat the oil in a flameproof casserole, add the onion and garlic and fry gently for 5 minutes until soft but not coloured.

2 Add the chicken portions and fry for a few minutes more, turning the chicken constantly so that the pieces become browned on all sides.

3 Warm the brandy gently in a small pan or ladle. Remove the casserole from the heat, pour in the brandy and set it alight with a match.

4 When the flames have died down, return the casserole to the heat and add the peppers and tomatoes. Fry over moderate heat for about 10 minutes, mashing the tomatoes down to a purée with a wooden spoon.

5 Pour in the wine and stock and bring slowly to boiling point. Lower the heat, add the rosemary and season to taste with salt and pepper, then cover and simmer for 30 minutes or until the chicken is cooked when pierced with a skewer. Taste and adjust the seasoning before serving. Garnish with sprigs of rosemary.

COOK'S TIP

Using brandy and wine together is a popular Spanish combination. The actual alcohol content is burnt off during the cooking, giving body and richness to the sauce.

CATALONIAN CHICKEN

SERVES 4-6

1.4 kg (3 lb) chicken, jointed into 8 pieces

115 g (4 oz) plus 1½ × 15 ml tbs plain flour

salt and pepper

50 g (2 oz) butter

3 × 15 ml tbs vegetable oil

12 button onions, skinned

1 garlic clove, skinned and finely chopped

300 ml (10 fl oz) chicken stock

2 × 15 ml tbs white wine (optional)

2 × 5 ml tsp tomato purée

12 chestnuts

225 g (8 oz) chorizo sausage

1 Dip the chicken joints in the 115 g (4 oz) flour, liberally seasoned with salt and pepper.

2 Heat the butter and 2 × 15 ml tbs oil in a frying pan, add the chicken joints and fry until well browned. Remove from pan and drain on absorbent kitchen paper.

3 Add the onions and garlic to the pan and fry for 5 minutes until brown, then transfer to a 2.1-2.4 lt (3½-4 pt) casserole.

4 Add the remaining flour to the frying pan and stir in the chicken stock, white wine and tomato purée. Bring to a simmer.

5 Place the chicken on top of the onions. Pour the stock over and season to taste with salt and pepper. Cover and cook in the oven at 180°C/350°F/Gas Mark 4 for 1 hour.

6 Pierce the brown outer skins of chestnuts with a sharp knife. Plunge into boiling water for 3-5 minutes. Peel off brown and inner skins from the nuts. Simmer gently in water for 35 minutes until cooked.

7 Fry the sausages in the remaining oil, then cut each into three. Add with the chestnuts to the chicken 10 minutes before the end of cooking.

Catalonian Chicken

CHICKEN WITH ALMONDS AND SAFFRON

SERVES 4

4 × 15 ml tbs olive oil
1 thick slice bread, crusts removed and diced
50 g (2 oz) blanched almonds
2 garlic cloves, skinned and crushed
pinch of cumin seeds
small bunch of parsley, stalks removed
1 × 5 ml tsp ground cinnamon
pinch of ground cloves
75 ml (3 fl oz) medium sherry
large pinch of saffron threads, soaked in 2 × 15 ml tbs boiling water
grated rind and juice of 1 lemon
1.4 kg (3 lb) chicken, jointed into 8 pieces
1 small onion, skinned and chopped
200 ml (7 fl oz) chicken stock
toasted almonds and flat-leaf parsley, to garnish

1 Heat 2 × 15 ml tbs oil in a large frying pan, add the bread, almonds, garlic and cumin and fry for 2-3 minutes until golden brown. Remove from the pan with a slotted spoon and transfer to a food processor. Add the parsley, cinnamon, cloves, sherry, soaked saffron and water and the lemon rind and juice to the processor and blend to form a smooth paste.

2 Add the remaining oil to the pan, then add the chicken and onion and fry over a moderate heat for 8-10 minutes until the chicken is golden brown on all sides and the onion is softened.

3 Spoon the almond sauce over the chicken in the pan. Add the stock and bring to the boil. Reduce the heat, cover and simmer very gently for 30 minutes until the chicken is cooked and the sauce thickened. Garnish with almonds and parsley.

SPANISH CHICKEN AND RICE

SERVES 4

1.4 kg (3 lb) chicken, jointed into 8 pieces
2 × 15 ml tbs flour
salt and pepper
4 × 15 ml tbs vegetable oil
1 onion, skinned and chopped
400 g can tomatoes
a little water
160 g can pimientos, drained and sliced
2 chicken stock cubes, crumbled
12 stuffed olives
175 g (6 oz) long-grain rice
225 g (8 oz) chorizo sausages, cut into 1 cm (½ in) slices
115 g (4 oz) frozen peas

1 Toss the chicken joints in the flour seasoned with salt and pepper. Heat the oil in a large saucepan, brown the chicken on all sides and remove. Add the onion and fry until golden brown.

2 Drain the tomatoes and add enough water to make the juice up to 450 ml (16 fl oz).

3 Return the chicken to the pan. Add the tomato juice, the tomatoes, pimientos, stock cubes, olives, rice and sausages. Season to taste.

4 Bring to the boil, then cover the pan tightly, lower the heat and simmer gently for 45 minutes, forking carefully through the rice occasionally to prevent it sticking.

5 Add the peas to the pan, cover again and simmer for a further 30 minutes until the chicken is tender. Taste and adjust seasoning before serving hot.

TOP Spanish Chicken and Rice
BOTTOM Chicken with Almonds and Saffron

SEVILLE ROAST DUCK

8 garlic cloves, skinned
two 1.6-1.8 kg (3½-4 lb) oven-ready duckling
1 large onion, skinned and sliced
sprigs of fresh thyme
salt and pepper
115 g (4 oz) pitted green olives, quartered
350 ml (12 fl oz) dry sherry
115 g (4 oz) carrot, peeled
3 × 15 ml tbs olive oil
2 × 15 ml tbs plain white flour
750 ml (1¼ pt) chicken stock
1 × 15 ml tbs tomato purée
orange slices, to garnish

1 Halve six garlic cloves and place inside the duckling with a few slices from the onion, small bunches of thyme and seasoning.

2 Prick the birds all over with a fork and place on wire racks over roasting tins. Bake at 200°C/400°F/Gas Mark 6 for 1½ hours. Allow to cool slightly.

Seville Roast Duck

3 Meanwhile, cover the olive quarters with 3 × 15 ml tbs sherry and leave to marinate. Roughly chop the remaining onion and carrot.

4 Heat the oil in a large flameproof casserole. Add the onion, carrot and 2 crushed garlic cloves. Cook over a moderate heat for about 5 minutes or until the vegetables begin to soften and lightly brown. Stir in the flour and cook, stirring for 1 minute. Mix in the stock, tomato purée and remaining sherry. Season to taste with salt and pepper. Tie a small bunch of thyme with string and add to the sauce. Bring to the boil, then simmer for about 10 minutes.

5 Joint each duckling into four pieces, discarding the backbone and any excess fat. Add to the sauce and bring back to the boil. Cover and bake for a further 45 minutes–1 hour at 180°C/350°F/Gas Mark 4 until cooked. Remove duckling and keep warm.

6 Strain the sauce into a saucepan. Add the olives and sherry and simmer for 5 minutes. Skim off fat and adjust the seasoning. Place duckling on a platter. Spoon the sauce over and garnish with orange slices.

PORK LOIN STUFFED WITH FIGS

SERVES 4

3 × 15 ml tbs olive oil
1 onion, skinned and finely chopped
2 garlic cloves, skinned and chopped
75 g (3 oz) fresh breadcrumbs
4 ready-to-eat dried figs, finely chopped
8 pitted green olives, finely chopped
25 g (1 oz) flaked almonds, toasted and chopped
1 × 15 ml tbs lemon juice
1 × 15 ml tbs chopped fresh parsley
1 egg yolk
salt and pepper
900 g (2 lb) boned loin of pork
sprigs of flat-leaf parsley, to garnish

1 Heat 2 × 15 ml tbs oil in a frying pan, add the onion and garlic, and gently fry until soft. Stir in the next seven ingredients and season with salt and pepper.

2 Remove the string from the pork and unroll the flap away from the fillet in the centre, cutting away any excess fat or meat if necessary. Spread about half the stuffing over the flat piece. Roll up, starting from the thick side. Tie at intervals with string.

3 Pour the remaining oil into a small roasting tin and add the pork. Roast at 200°C/400°F/Gas Mark 6 for about 1 hour 15 minutes.

4 Shape the remaining stuffing into walnut-sized balls and add to the roasting tin 15-20 minutes before the end of the cooking time.

5 Remove the pork and stuffing balls from oven. Allow meat to rest for 10 minutes before slicing. Serve garnished with parsley sprigs.

Pork Loin Stuffed with Figs

ASTURIAN PORK AND BEAN CASSEROLE

SERVES 6-8

900 g (2 lb) shoulder of ham or gammon joint
115 g (4 oz) dried haricot beans
115 g (4 oz) dried butter beans
1 × 15 ml tbs olive oil
*50 g (2 oz) streaky bacon, rinded and cut
into thin strips*
2 garlic cloves, skinned and crushed
2 Spanish onions, skinned and sliced
225 g (8 oz) leeks, washed, trimmed and sliced
1 carrot, peeled and chopped
1 bay leaf
1 × 5 ml tsp paprika
salt and pepper
*115 g (4 oz) chorizo or other spicy sausage,
cut into 2.5 cm (1 in) lengths*
115 g (4 oz) black pudding, sliced
bay leaves, to garnish

1 Soak the ham overnight in enough cold water to cover. In a separate bowl, soak the haricot beans and butter beans in enough cold water to cover.

2 Drain the soaked ham. Drain the soaked beans and rinse thoroughly under cold running water. Place the beans in a pan of water and boil rapidly for 10 minutes, then drain.

3 Heat the oil in a large flameproof casserole, add the bacon and cook gently for 2-3 minutes, then stir in the garlic, onions, leeks and carrot and continue cooking for 10 minutes.

4 Stir in the drained beans with the bay leaf and paprika. Cover with cold water and season with salt and pepper to taste. Bring to the boil, then lower the heat, cover and simmer for 30 minutes. Add the ham or gammon and simmer for a further hour.

5 Add the chorizo sausage and black pudding

and simmer gently for a further 20-25 minutes.

6 Allow to cool slightly, then remove the ham with a slotted spoon. Remove the fat and any string from the ham, then cut into bite-sized pieces and return to the casserole. Discard the bay leaf. Reheat gently and serve hot, garnished with fresh bay leaves.

LAMB WITH GARLIC AND BEANS

SERVES 6

3 × 15 ml tbs olive oil
1.4 kg (3 lb) boned lamb, cut into 5 cm (2 in) cubes
1 large onion, skinned and chopped
6 large garlic cloves, unpeeled
1 bay leaf
1 × 5 ml tsp paprika
115 ml (4 fl oz) sherry or red wine vinegar
salt and pepper
115 g (4 oz) frozen broad beans
2 × 15 ml tbs chopped fresh parsley

1 Heat 2 × 15 ml tbs of the oil in a large flameproof casserole. Add the meat, in batches if necessary, and brown well on all sides. Remove from pan, using a slotted spoon and reserve. Add the onion, and gently fry until soft. Return the meat to the casserole.

2 Stir in the garlic cloves, bay leaf, paprika and vinegar. Season to taste with salt and pepper. Cover and cook over a low heat for 1½-2 hours, until the meat is tender.

3 Ten minutes before the end of cooking time, add the broad beans. Stir in the chopped parsley just before serving.

TOP Asturian Pork and Bean Casserole
BOTTOM Lamb with Garlic and Beans

BEEF WITH HAZELNUTS AND PEARS

SERVES 4

50 g (2 oz) hazelnuts
4 × 15 ml tbs olive oil
675 g (1½ lb) braising steak, cut into large pieces
150 ml (5 fl oz) white Rioja wine
3 pears, peeled, cored and quartered
1 cinnamon stick
2 garlic cloves, skinned and crushed
1 × 15 ml tbs plain flour
150 ml (5 fl oz) beef stock
salt and pepper
4 tomatoes, skinned and chopped

1 Spread out the hazelnuts in a baking tin and bake in the oven at 180°C/350°F/Gas Mark 4 for about 15 minutes until golden brown. Leave to cool, then work in a food processor until finely ground. Set aside.

2 Heat the oil in a large shallow pan and fry the beef over a high heat for about 5 minutes until well browned on all sides. While the beef is cooking, pour the wine into a separate saucepan, add the pears and cinnamon stick and simmer for 5-8 minutes until tender. Set aside.

3 When the beef is browned, add the garlic and flour and cook, stirring, for 1-2 minutes. Strain the liquid from the pears into the pan, add the stock and salt and pepper to taste and bring to the boil. Cover the pan and simmer for about 1¼-1½ hours or until the beef is tender.

4 Stir in the tomatoes and hazelnuts and cook for 2-3 minutes until the tomatoes are beginning to soften. Add the pears and heat through gently. Serve hot.

KIDNEYS IN SHERRY SAUCE

SERVES 4

16 lambs' kidneys, total weight about 900 g (2 lb)
salt and pepper
2 × 15 ml tbs olive oil
2 onions, skinned and finely chopped
2 garlic cloves, skinned and crushed
2 × 15 ml tbs chopped fresh parsley
3 × 15 ml tbs plain flour
350 ml (12 fl oz) dry sherry
350 ml (12 fl oz) beef stock
chopped fresh parsley, to garnish

1 Cut the kidneys in half. Remove the cores and fat, then cut each in half again. Sprinkle with salt and pepper.

2 Heat the oil in a large frying pan and fry the kidneys over a high heat for 1 minute. Transfer to a warm dish. Using the same pan, add the onion, garlic and parsley and gently fry until soft. Stir in the flour and cook for 1 minute. Add the sherry and stock, stirring continuously until thickened and smooth. Cover and simmer gently for 10 minutes.

3 Return the kidneys to the pan and simmer for a further 5-10 minutes. Serve hot, garnished with chopped parsley.

COOK'S TIP

Be careful not to overcook the kidneys or they will become tough. The insides should be just pale pink. If you prefer a smooth sauce, sieve the sauce before returning the kidneys to the pan in step 3.

Kidneys in Sherry Sauce

COUNTRY-STYLE RABBIT CASSEROLE

SERVES 6

3 × 15 ml tbs olive oil
1.25 kg (2½ lb) rabbit pieces
1 large onion, skinned and sliced
2 garlic cloves, skinned and crushed
115 g (4 oz) lean smoked bacon, diced
2 × 15 ml tbs brandy
200 ml (7 fl oz) white wine
400 g can chopped tomatoes
½ × 5 ml tsp dried thyme
1 × 15 ml tbs chopped fresh parsley
salt and pepper
50 g (2 oz) brown cap mushrooms, wiped clean and sliced
crusty bread, to serve
chopped flat-leaf parsley, to garnish

1 Heat the oil in a heavy-based flameproof casserole. Add the rabbit pieces and brown well on all sides. Remove with a slotted spoon.

2 Add the onion, garlic and bacon to the casserole. Gently fry until the onion has softened. Return the rabbit to the casserole.

3 Warm the brandy gently in a small pan or ladle. Remove the casserole from the heat, pour the brandy over the rabbit and set it alight with a match.

4 When the flames have died down, return the casserole to the heat and add the wine, tomatoes, thyme and parsley. Season with salt and pepper. Cover and simmer over a low heat for about 1½ hours, adding the mushrooms 10 minutes before the end of the cooking time. Serve the casserole with crusty bread and garnish with chopped parsley.

TARRAGON ORANGE VEAL

SERVES 4

4 veal escalopes, each weighing about 115 g (4 oz)
2 × 15 ml tbs plain flour
salt and pepper
1 × 15 ml tbs olive oil
1 onion, skinned and roughly chopped
2 garlic cloves, skinned and thinly sliced
25 g (1 oz) butter
115 ml (4 fl oz) fresh orange juice
1 × 15 ml tbs lemon juice
1 × 15 ml tbs chopped fresh tarragon
sprigs of tarragon and orange rind shreds, to garnish

1 Place the veal escalopes between two pieces of cling film. Using a wooden rolling pin, pound them to a thickness of about 0.3 cm (⅛ in). If they are very large, cut them into manageable pieces. Coat in the flour, seasoned with salt and pepper.

2 Heat the oil in a frying pan, add the onion and garlic and fry gently until softened. Remove with a slotted spoon and set aside. Add the butter to the pan and heat. When the butter stops sizzling, add the veal, in batches if necessary, and fry for 1 minute on each side. Return the onion and garlic to the pan with the orange and lemon juice. Simmer for a few seconds, turning the veal in the juice.

3 Add the tarragon and season to taste with salt and pepper. Remove from the heat and serve immediately, garnished with tarragon sprigs and orange rind shreds.

Country-style Rabbit Casserole

FISH AND SHELLFISH DISHES

Due to the vast coastline of Spain, fish and shellfish play an important role in the cuisine of the country. Dried salt cod is particularly associated with Spanish cooking and is popular cooked casserole-style with vegetables and wine. Shellfish, too, crops up in many dishes and prawns served with a piquant almond and tomato sauce is typically Spanish. Equally Spanish is the renowned rice dish paella and here you will find a tasty all-seafood version, as well as a really appetizing tuna and spinach pie.

OPPOSITE
TOP Spinach and Tuna Empanada
BOTTOM Bacalao Vegetable Casserole

47

HADDOCK AND PRAWN PAELLA

SERVES 8

450 g (1 lb) tomatoes, skinned

good pinch of saffron strands

150 ml (5 fl oz) boiling water

6 × 15 ml tbs olive oil

2 large onions, skinned and chopped

450 g (1 lb) long-grain white rice

about 600 ml (1 pt) fish stock

300 ml (10 fl oz) dry white wine

675 g (1½ lb) fresh haddock fillet, skinned and cut into chunks

1 yellow and 1 green pepper, seeded and cut into bite-sized pieces

2 × 15 ml tbs chopped fresh thyme

1 garlic clove, skinned and crushed

salt and pepper

225 g (8 oz) cooked shelled mussels

225 g (8 oz) peeled prawns

sprigs of fresh thyme, to garnish

1 Quarter and de-seed the tomatoes. Sieve the pulp, reserving the juices.
2 Place the saffron in a heatproof jug, pour on the boiling water. Leave to soak for about 10 minutes, then strain, reserving the liquid.
3 Heat the oil in a large flameproof casserole. Add the onions and fry over moderate heat until just brown. Stir in the rice, stock, wine and saffron liquid. Bring to the boil, stirring.
4 Gently mix in the haddock chunks, peppers, tomato and reserved tomato juices, thyme and garlic and season to taste with salt and pepper. Cover the casserole tightly.
5 Bake in the oven at 180°C/350°F/Gas Mark 4 for 20 minutes. Carefully stir in the mussels and prawns. Cover again and bake for 10 minutes or until the rice is quite tender and all the liquid is absorbed.
6 Adjust the seasoning and serve the paella immediately, garnished with thyme sprigs.

BACALAO VEGETABLE CASSEROLE

SERVES 4

450 g (1 lb) salt cod

25 g (1 oz) plain flour

4 × 15 ml tbs olive oil

2 onions, skinned and chopped

1 large aubergine, peeled and cut into 4 cm (1½ in) dice

1 green and 1 yellow pepper, seeded and cut into strips

400 g can chopped tomatoes

90 ml (3½ fl oz) white wine

salt and pepper

lemon slices and green salad, to garnish

1 Soak the salt cod for 24 hours in cold water, changing the water three or four times. Drain then put in a pot with enough fresh water to cover. Bring to the boil, then immediately remove from the heat.
2 Drain the cod and break into 4 cm (1½ in) pieces, removing any skin and bones. Dust with the flour.
3 Heat the oil in a large, shallow, flameproof casserole and fry the fish until golden. Using a slotted spoon, remove from the dish and set aside.
4 Add the onions, aubergine and peppers to the casserole and gently fry for about 10 minutes until soft. Add the tomatoes and wine, and season with salt and pepper. Simmer, covered, for 20 minutes. Add the cod and cook for a further 10 minutes. Serve hot, garnished with lemon slices and green salad.

COOK'S TIP

Start the dish the day before you plan to eat it.

Haddock and Prawn Paella

GRILLED PRAWNS WITH ROMESCO SAUCE

SERVES 4

6 × 15 ml tbs olive oil
1 onion, skinned and finely chopped
4 garlic cloves, skinned and chopped
2 ripe tomatoes
1 canned pimiento, chopped
½ × 5 ml tsp crushed dried chilli
5 × 15 ml tbs fish stock
2 × 15 ml tbs white wine
10 blanched almonds, lightly toasted
1 × 15 ml tbs red wine vinegar
salt
32 raw shell on tiger prawns
tomato strips and toasted almonds, to garnish

1 To make the sauce, heat 2 × 15 ml tbs of the olive oil in a saucepan. Add the onion and garlic and gently fry until soft.

2 Plunge the tomatoes into boiling water for 30 seconds. Remove and put into cold water. Peel off the skins and chop roughly. Add to the onion together with the pimiento, chilli, fish stock and white wine. Simmer, covered, for 30 minutes.

3 Grind the almonds in a food processor or blender. Add 2 × 15 ml tbs oil, the vinegar and salt to taste, then blend again. Add the tomato and pimiento mixture, and blend until smooth. Set aside until ready to serve.

4 Remove the heads from the prawns. Rinse in cold water and dry on absorbent kitchen paper. Toss the prawns in the remaining olive oil, arrange in a single layer in a grill pan and grill for 2-3 minutes each side until pink. Garnish with tomato and almonds and serve with the sauce.

Grilled Prawns with Romesco Sauce

SCALLOPS IN TOMATO WINE SAUCE

SERVES 3–4

450 g (1 lb) frozen queen scallops, thawed

25 g (1 oz) butter

2 × 15 ml tbs olive oil

3 salad onions, trimmed and finely sliced

2 garlic cloves, skinned and crushed

½ dried red chilli, finely chopped

6 tomatoes, skinned, seeded and cut into thin strips

3 × 15 ml tbs white wine or stock

2 × 15 ml tbs tomato purée

salt and pepper

tomato strips, to garnish

Scallops in Tomato Wine Sauce

1 Cut off the orange corals from the scallops and set aside. Slice the white scallop flesh in half and set aside. Heat the butter and the oil in a small frying pan and gently fry the salad onions for 2 minutes. Add the white pieces of scallop and cook for 2-3 minutes, turning once, then add the corals and cook for 30 seconds.

2 Stir in the garlic, chilli and tomatoes and cook for 1 minute. Mix together the wine and tomato purée and add to the pan with salt and pepper to taste. Allow to boil and thicken, then serve at once, garnished with tomato strips.

SPINACH AND TUNA EMPANADA

SERVES 6

450 g (1 lb) plain flour
1½ × 5 ml tsp salt
1 sachet fast-action dried yeast
40 g (1½ oz) lard or white vegetable fat melted
2 eggs, beaten
115 ml (4 fl oz) milk, warmed
450 g (1 lb) fresh spinach, washed and trimmed
3 × 15 ml tbs olive oil
1 garlic clove, skinned and finely chopped
355 g can tuna chunks in brine, drained
salt and pepper
115 g (4 oz) Gouda cheese, diced

1 Sift the flour and salt together into a large bowl. Stir in the yeast. Make a well in the centre, and add the cooled lard and eggs. Gradually stir in the milk, drawing the flour and liquid together to form a dough. Knead for 2-3 minutes, then return the dough to the bowl. Cover and leave in a warm place for about 1½ hours.

2 Put the wet spinach into a large saucepan and cook, covered, over a high heat until wilted. Squeeze out excess moisture and roughly chop.

3 Heat the oil in a pan, add the spinach and garlic and cook for 5 minutes. Stir in the tuna and season to taste with salt and pepper. Set aside.

4 Knead the dough for 2-3 minutes and return to the bowl. Cover and leave for 1 hour.

5 Knock back the dough and cut in half. Roll out one half to a circle about 28 cm (11 in) in diameter and place on a baking tray. Spread the spinach mixture over the dough, leaving a 2.5 cm (1 in) border. Sprinkle with the cheese. Roll out the remaining dough to the same size. Brush the border with a little water and place on top of the filling. Crimp the edges to seal and make several slits in the dough.

6 Bake at 180°C/350°F/Gas Mark 4 for 20-25 minutes until a pale golden. Serve hot.

WHITING AND COCKLES IN SALSA VERDE

SERVES 4

4 whiting fillets, skinned
salt and pepper
1 × 15 ml tbs lemon juice
2 × 15 ml tbs olive oil
1 small onion, skinned and very finely chopped
4 garlic cloves, skinned and crushed
2 × 15 ml tbs plain flour
150 ml (5 fl oz) white wine
150 ml (5 fl oz) fish stock
6 × 15 ml tbs chopped fresh parsley
75 g (3 oz) frozen petits pois
198 g jar cockles in brine, drained and rinsed

1 Season the fish with salt and pepper. Arrange in an ovenproof dish and sprinkle with lemon juice.

2 Heat the oil in a large frying pan. Add the onion and garlic and gently fry until softened. Stir in the flour and cook for 1 minute. Gradually add the wine and stock, stirring until thickened and smooth. Add 5 × 15 ml tbs of parsley and the peas. Season to taste with salt and pepper.

3 Scatter the cockles over the fish, then pour the sauce over. Bake at 200°C/400°F/Gas Mark 6 for about 20 minutes until the fish is cooked through. Sprinkle with the remaining parsley before serving.

COOK'S TIP

You may prefer to cook this dish in four individual gratin dishes. In which case, cut the fillets into large pieces, distribute between the dishes, then top with the cockles and sauce.

Whiting and Cockles in Salsa Verde

VEGETABLE DISHES
AND SALADS

Bright-red tomatoes and glossy peppers are used extensively in Spanish cooking and in this chapter you will find a range of colourful dishes which make use of these distinctive ingredients. Peppers filled with an anchovy-flavoured stuffing or stewed with chick-peas make delicious Spanish-style supper dishes, while tomatoes baked with spinach or tossed into a salad of oranges and asparagus provide memorable side-dishes. Artichoke hearts, aubergines and olives are also used imaginatively to create unusual and exciting vegetable accompaniments.

STUFFED PEPPERS

SERVES 4

4 red, green or yellow peppers
2 × 15 ml tbs olive oil, plus a little for drizzling
1 small onion, skinned and chopped
1 garlic clove, skinned and chopped
75 g (3 oz) pine kernels or chopped almonds
200 g (7 oz) fresh breadcrumbs
75 g (3 oz) sultanas
2 × 15 ml tbs chopped fresh parsley
50 g (2 oz) can anchovy fillets, drained and chopped
1 × 5 ml tsp sugar
1 × 5 ml tsp lemon juice
salt and pepper
a little water
juice of 1 orange
50 g (2 oz) Gouda cheese, thinly sliced

1 Cut the peppers in half lengthways. Remove the cores and seeds but leave the stalks intact.

2 Heat the oil in a frying pan. Add the onion and garlic and cook for 8-10 minutes until soft and golden. Add the pine kernels or almonds and breadcrumbs. Continue to cook, stirring, until the ingredients are browned.

3 Remove from the heat and stir in the sultanas, parsley, anchovies, sugar, lemon juice and salt and pepper to taste.

4 Pile the mixture into the pepper halves and place in a roasting tin or ovenproof dish. Pour in just enough water to cover the bottom of the dish by about 0.6 cm (¼ in) and drizzle the peppers with a little olive oil. Cook at 190°C/375°F/Gas Mark 5 for 30-40 minutes.

5 Ten to fifteen minutes before the end of cooking time, pour the orange juice over the peppers. Place the cheese slices on top of the stuffing. Return the peppers to the oven and cook until the cheese has melted.

GARBANZO STEW

SERVES 6

1 × 15 ml tbs olive oil
1 large onion, skinned and chopped
1 red pepper, seeded and chopped
2 garlic cloves, skinned and crushed
400 g can chopped tomatoes
2 × 430 g cans chick-peas, drained and rinsed
salt and pepper
chopped flat-leaf parsley and paprika, to garnish

1 Heat the oil in a heavy-based saucepan. Add the onion, pepper and garlic and cook over a high heat for 2 minutes. Add the tomatoes and simmer for 5 minutes.

2 Add the chick-peas to the tomato sauce. Cover and simmer for about 10 minutes, stirring occasionally. Season to taste with salt and pepper and garnish with parsley and a sprinkling of paprika. Serve warm.

COOK'S TIP

This really easy dish is also delicious served with boiled rice for a more substantial supper dish. Chorizo sausage too makes a tasty addition to the stew: cut a 335 g (12 oz) piece of it into chunky pieces and add with the chick-peas at step 2.

Garbanzo Stew

FRIED AUBERGINE STRIPS

SERVES 4

1 large aubergine, weighing about 335 g (12 oz)
salt
300 ml (10 fl oz) olive oil
300 ml (10 fl oz) sunflower oil
plain flour, for dusting
flakes or crystals of sea salt, to serve
flat-leaf parsley, to garnish

1 Cut the aubergine lengthways into thin strips, about 0.3 cm (⅛ in) thick. Place the strips in layers in a colander, sprinkling with salt between each layer. Leave to drain for at least 30 minutes.

2 Rinse the aubergine slices under cold running water and dry thoroughly on absorbent kitchen paper.

3 Heat the olive oil and sunflower oil together in a deep frying pan.

4 Dust the aubergine slices with flour and fry in the hot oil, 2 or 3 at a time, until golden. Drain on absorbent kitchen paper, sprinkle with flakes or crystals of sea salt and serve immediately, garnished with parsley.

SPICY POTATOES

SERVES 4-6

675 g (1½ lb) waxy potatoes, scrubbed
2 × 15 ml tbs olive oil
2 garlic cloves, skinned and chopped
1 green chilli, seeded and chopped
1 × 5 ml tsp mild paprika
400 g can chopped tomatoes
salt and pepper
chopped fresh parsley, to garnish

1 Cook the potatoes in boiling salted water until just tender. Drain and leave to cool.

2 Meanwhile, heat the oil in a deep frying pan, add the garlic, chilli and paprika and gently fry for 2 minutes, stirring all the time. Add the tomatoes, increase the heat and simmer for about 10 minutes until the sauce is reduced and very thick.

3 Carefully peel the potatoes, and cut into large chunks. Add to the tomato sauce and cook for about 10 minutes, stirring occasionally, until the sauce is reduced further and just clings to the potato. Season to taste with salt and pepper. Serve warm or cold, sprinkled generously with parsley.

Fried Aubergine Strips

Baked Tomato Salad with Baby Spinach Leaves

BAKED TOMATO SALAD WITH BABY SPINACH LEAVES

SERVES 4

3 beefsteak tomatoes, cut into wedges

4 × 15 ml tbs extra-virgin olive oil

1 onion, skinned and sliced into rings

6 sun-dried tomatoes, finely sliced

12 black olives, stoned

small handful of flat-leaf parsley, coarsely chopped

salt and pepper

115 g (4 oz) baby spinach leaves

1 Arrange the tomato wedges skin-side down in a baking dish. Heat the oil in a frying pan, add the onion and fry for 3-5 minutes until softened. Lift out the onion rings with a slotted spoon and arrange on top of the tomatoes.

2 Scatter over the sun-dried tomatoes, olives and half of the parsley and season well with salt and pepper. Drizzle with the oil from the pan and bake in the oven at 200°C/400°F/Gas Mark 6 for 15-20 minutes, basting occasionally, until the tomatoes are just tender. Scatter the remaining parsley over and leave to cool.

3 When ready to serve, arrange the spinach on serving plates, place the tomatoes on top, drizzle with the juices from the baking dish and serve.

POTATO AND ROSEMARY CAKE

SERVES 6

3 × 15 ml tbs olive oil
450 g (1 lb) onions, skinned and sliced
900 g (2 lb) new potatoes
2 garlic cloves, skinned and crushed
2 × 15 ml tbs chopped fresh rosemary
salt and pepper
300 ml (10 fl oz) single cream

1 Heat the oil in a saucepan. Add the onions, cover and gently fry over a moderate heat for about 30 minutes or until very soft and lightly browned. Stir once or twice.

2 Cut the potatoes into thin slices (but not the wafer-thin type that a food processor would produce).

3 Lightly oil a 1.8 lt (3 pt) shallow ovenproof dish. Layer the potatoes, onions, crushed garlic, rosemary and seasoning, ending with potatoes and a sprinkling of rosemary. Pour the cream over and lightly press down the potatoes until they are almost submerged in the mixture. Cover the dish loosely with foil.

4 Place on a baking tray and bake at 200°C/400°F/Gas Mark 6 for 1 hour. Uncover and continue to bake at 180°C/350°F/Gas Mark 4 for a further 30 minutes or until the potatoes are quite tender and the top golden brown. Serve hot.

ARTICHOKES WITH POTATOES AND THYME

SERVES 6

675 g (1½ lb) large new potatoes, scrubbed and cut lengthways into wedges
salt and pepper
3 × 15 ml tbs olive oil
3 garlic cloves, skinned and finely sliced
2 × 400 g (14 oz) cans artichoke hearts, drained and halved
3 × 15 ml tbs chopped fresh thyme
grated rind and juice of 2 small lemons

1 Cook the potatoes in a saucepan of boiling salted water for 5 minutes, then drain. Heat the oil in a frying pan, add the potatoes and fry for 3-5 minutes over a high heat until browned, stirring frequently.

2 Stir in the garlic and the halved artichoke hearts and fry for about 2 minutes. Add the thyme, lemon rind and juice and season liberally to taste with salt and pepper. Heat through and serve at once, or leave to cool.

COOK'S TIP

New potatoes work particularly well in this dish as they hold their shape and do not become 'floury' during cooking. Use large potatoes of similar size to ensure that they cook evenly when cut into wedges.

Potato and Rosemary Cake

VEGETARIAN PAELLA

SERVES 4

3 × 15 ml tbs olive oil
1 onion, skinned and chopped
1 garlic clove, skinned and crushed
300 g (11 oz) Arborio risotto rice
900 ml (1½ pt) vegetable stock
150 ml (5 fl oz) dry white wine
3 small carrots, peeled and sliced diagonally
225 g (8 oz) frozen broad beans
salt and pepper
115 g (4 oz) asparagus tips
175 g (6 oz) sugar snap peas or mange-tout, trimmed
175 g (6 oz) cherry tomatoes, halved
4 × 15 ml tbs chopped fresh parsley

1 Heat the oil in a large heavy-based shallow pan, add the onion and fry for 3-5 minutes until softened. Stir in the garlic and rice and cook for 2 minutes, stirring to coat the grains in oil.

2 Mix together the stock and wine, then add 150 ml (5 fl oz) of the stock mixture to the rice. Simmer over a low heat, stirring occasionally until the liquid is absorbed. Add the carrots with 300 ml (10 fl oz) of the stock mixture and continue cooking until the liquid is absorbed.

3 Stir in the broad beans and 150 ml (5 fl oz) of the stock mixture and cook until the liquid is absorbed. Adjust the seasoning and add the asparagus and sugar snap peas to the pan with another 150 ml (5 fl oz) of the stock mixture and cook until the liquid is absorbed. Add the remaining stock mixture and cook for about 25 minutes or until the liquid is absorbed and the rice is tender.

4 Gently stir in the tomatoes and parsley, cover the pan and leave to stand for 5 minutes before serving.

SAFFRON AND OLIVE RICE

SERVES 4

600 ml (20 fl oz) vegetable stock
½ × 5 ml tsp saffron threads
2 × 15 ml tbs olive oil
4 shallots, skinned and finely chopped
2 garlic cloves, skinned and crushed
225 g (8 oz) long-grain rice
2 or 3 sprigs fresh thyme
75 g (3 oz) frozen petits pois
25 g (1 oz) pitted green olives, chopped
25 g (1 oz) pitted black olives, chopped
salt and pepper

1 Bring the vegetable stock to the boil with the saffron threads. Remove from the heat and leave for 5 minutes for the flavour to infuse.

2 Heat the oil in a pan. Add the shallots and garlic and gently fry until softened.

3 Add the rice, stirring until the grains are coated in oil. Add the saffron-flavoured stock and the thyme sprigs. Bring to the boil, cover and simmer for about 12 minutes.

4 Add the peas 4-5 minutes before the end of the cooking time, leaving them on top of the mixture to cook.

5 Stir in the olives and season to taste with salt and pepper. Serve hot.

TOP Saffron and Olive Rice
BOTTOM Vegetarian Paella

SPICED EGG SALAD

SERVES 4

5 × 15 ml tbs olive oil
2 × 15 ml tbs red wine vinegar
1 × 5 ml tsp paprika
½ × 5 ml tsp ground cumin
1 large garlic clove, skinned and crushed
salt and pepper
1 small head escarole, Chinese leaves or other salad leaves
50 g (2 oz) pitted black olives
4 hard-boiled eggs, cut into wedges

1 Whisk together the first six ingredients.
2 Rinse and drain the salad leaves. Pat dry with absorbent kitchen paper then tear into shreds.
3 Just before serving, arrange the leaves on a flat platter. Add the olives and wedges of hard-boiled egg. Spoon the dressing over the salad and serve immediately.

MARINATED COURGETTES

SERVES 6-8

900 g (2 lb) courgettes
salt and pepper
about 6 × 15 ml tbs olive oil
8 large garlic cloves, skinned and thinly sliced
2 × 15 ml tbs chopped fresh mint
4 × 15 ml tbs balsamic or red wine vinegar

1 Wipe and trim the courgettes. Cut lengthways into strips about 6 cm (2½ in) long and 0.6 cm (¼ in) thick. Place on a large, non-metallic dish, sprinkle with salt and leave for 30 minutes. Rinse and pat dry on absorbent kitchen paper.
2 Heat the oil in a large non-stick frying pan.

Add the garlic and fry over a moderate heat until well browned. Drain on absorbent kitchen paper.
3 Add the courgettes to the pan and fry quickly in batches until golden brown on both sides. Drain on absorbent kitchen paper.
4 Place the courgettes, mint and garlic in layers in a non-metallic dish, seasoning the layers with pepper. Spoon the vinegar over the courgettes. Cover and marinate in the refrigerator for 3-4 hours, pressing down and basting occasionally.
5 Leave to stand at room temperature for about 30 minutes before serving.

ASPARAGUS AND ORANGE SALAD

SERVES 4

225 g (8 oz) asparagus, sliced into 5 cm (2 in) lengths
salt and pepper
2 oranges
2 ripe tomatoes, sliced into segments
50 g (2 oz) watercress, trimmed, washed and dried
2 × 15 ml tbs olive oil
½ × 5 ml tsp red wine vinegar
orange rind shreds, to garnish

1 Cook the asparagus in boiling, salted water for 3-4 minutes until tender. Drain and cool.
2 Finely grate the rind from half an orange and reserve. Peel the oranges and cut into segments. Squeeze the juice from the membrane; reserve.
3 Place the tomatoes and watercress in a salad bowl with the asparagus and orange segments.
4 Whisk the olive oil and vinegar with 1 × 15 ml tbs of the reserved orange juice and 1 × 5 ml tsp of rind. Season with salt and pepper.
5 Pour the dressing over the salad and mix gently. Garnish with orange rind shreds.

Asparagus and Orange Salad

SWEET TREATS

Round off a meal on a heady note with a luscious Spanish-style dessert. Choose a puff pastry tart filled with apricots and pine kernels to capture the true taste of Spain, or treat guests to a wickedly rich chocolate slice, flavoured with nuts and figs. If you prefer a fresh and fruity finale, try strawberries puréed with sherry or grilled fruit kebabs marinated in a luxurious orange liqueur syrup. As an indulgent treat to serve with coffee, crisp Churros and little almond cookies are totally irresistible.

OPPOSITE
TOP Apple Tart
BOTTOM Grilled Fruit Kebabs

CATALAN TART

SERVES 8

2 × 410 g cans apricots in apple and
apricot juice

25 g (1 oz) caster sugar

213 g packet puff pastry

2 eggs, beaten

115 g (4 oz) pine kernels

1 × 5 ml tsp ground cinnamon

1 Drain the apricots and place in a heavy-based saucepan with 150 ml (5 fl oz) of the juice. Add the sugar and cook over moderate heat for 15 minutes, stirring frequently until the apricots have softened to a thick purée. Take care, as the mixture will splutter as it thickens.

2 Meanwhile, roll out the pastry to a 30 × 15 cm (12 × 6 in) rectangle, then carefully cut a 3 cm (1¼ in) wide border around the edge. Remove the central piece of pastry and roll out to a 30 × 15 cm (12 × 6 in) rectangle.

3 Transfer the pastry rectangle to a baking tray and prick all over a with a fork. Dampen the edge of the rectangle and lay the border on top. Brush the border with a little of the beaten egg, then mark into diamond shapes using the point of a sharp knife. Chill for 10 minutes.

4 Spread out the pine kernels on a baking tray and bake in the oven at 200°C/400°F/Gas Mark 6 for 10 minutes, then remove from the oven. Bake the pastry case for 25-30 minutes until the sides are well risen and golden brown, then remove from the oven. Reduce the oven temperature to 180°C/350°F/Gas Mark 4.

5 Mix the remaining beaten eggs with the cinnamon and two-thirds of the pine kernels and beat into the apricot mixture, then spoon into the pastry case and spread evenly. Scatter the remaining pine kernels over the top and bake for 30 minutes. Serve warm.

SANTIAGO ALMOND TARTS

SERVES 6

335 g (12 oz) prepared shortcrust pastry

115 g (4 oz) unsalted butter

150 g (5 oz) caster sugar

finely grated rind of 2 lemons

2 eggs

2 × 15 ml tbs plain flour

6 × 15 ml tbs water

2 × 15 ml tbs brandy

175 g (6 oz) ground almonds

50 g (2 oz) flaked almonds

2 × 15 ml tbs icing sugar

1 Roll out the pastry thinly and use to line six 10 cm (4 in) fluted flan tins. Line the pastry cases with greaseproof paper and weigh down with baking beans. Place on a baking tray and bake in the oven at 200°C/400°F/Gas Mark 6 for 10 minutes. Remove the lining paper and beans and return the pastry cases to the oven for 5 minutes to dry out. Lower the oven temperature to 180°C/350°F/Gas Mark 4.

2 Beat together the butter and sugar until light and fluffy, then beat in the lemon rind. Beat in the eggs, one at a time, beating well after each addition and adding the flour with the final egg. Stir in the water, brandy and ground almonds.

3 Spoon the filling into the pastry cases, spread evenly and scatter the flaked almonds over the top. Place on a hot baking tray and bake for 30-35 minutes, or until the filling is springy to the touch. Leave to cool, then turn out of the tins and sprinkle with icing sugar.

TOP Catalan Tart
BOTTOM Santiago Almond Tarts

APPLE TART

SERVES 6–8

PASTRY
175 g (6 oz) plain flour
pinch of salt
115 g (4 oz) butter
2 × 15 ml tbs icing sugar
2-3 × 15 ml tbs cold water
ground cinnamon, to decorate (optional)
FILLING
50 g (2 oz) sugar
1 × 5 ml tsp lemon juice
½ × 5 ml tsp ground cinnamon
3 small dessert apples, peeled, cored and thinly sliced
300 ml (10 fl oz) fresh custard sauce
8 × 15 ml tbs apricot jam

1 To make the pastry, sift the flour and salt together. Rub in the butter until the mixture resembles fine breadcrumbs. Stir in the sugar, then mix in 2 × 15 ml tbs water to make a dough, adding a little more water, if necessary. Roll out on a floured surface and use to line a 23 cm (9 in) loose-bottom flan tin. Chill for 30 minutes.

2 Line the pastry case with greaseproof paper, and fill with baking beans. Bake at 200°C/400°F/Gas Mark 6 for 10-15 minutes. Remove the lining paper and beans and return to the oven for 5 minutes to dry out. Leave to cool.

3 Mix together the sugar, lemon juice, cinnamon and apples. Spread the custard over the pastry and arrange the apple slices on top. Bake at 180°C/350°F/Gas Mark 4 for about 45 minutes until golden.

4 Melt the apricot jam, then sieve and brush over the apple slices. Allow the tart to cool completely, then chill before removing from the tin. Chill until ready to serve. Sprinkle with a little cinnamon to decorate if wished.

NUTTY FIG AND CHOCOLATE SLICE

SERVES 6-8

175 g (6 oz) flaked hazelnuts
175 g (6 oz) plain chocolate, broken into squares
335 g (12 oz) ready-to-eat dried figs, coarsely chopped
1 × 15 ml tbs icing sugar (optional)

1 Spread out the hazelnuts on a baking tray and bake in the oven at 180°C/350°F/Gas Mark 4 for 10 minutes until golden brown. Meanwhile, place the chocolate in a small heat-proof bowl set over a pan of simmering water to melt.

2 Place the figs in a food processor, add the chocolate and two-thirds of the hazelnuts and process until well mixed, but not completely smooth.

3 Line the base of an 18 cm (7 in) square baking tin with non-stick baking parchment and carefully spoon the chocolate mixture over. Spread evenly using a palette knife, then scatter the remaining hazelnuts on top and press down lightly. Chill for 15 minutes.

4 Invert onto a board to unmould, carefully remove the lining paper, then quickly turn on to a second board. Sift the icing sugar, if using, over the top and cut into little rectangles or squares using a sharp knife.

Nutty Fig and Chocolate Slice

GRILLED FRUIT KEBABS

SERVES 4

50 g (2 oz) caster sugar
4 × 15 ml tbs orange-flavoured liqueur
finely grated rind and juice of 1 large orange
2 small oranges
1 small pineapple
2 bananas

1 Place the sugar and liqueur in a small saucepan and heat gently until the sugar has dissolved. Remove from the heat and stir in the orange rind and juice. Leave to cool.

2 Meanwhile, cut each small orange into eight wedges. Cut off the top and base of the pineapple, then cut lengthways into four slices. Cut each slice into four chunks. Place the pineapple and orange in a non-metallic bowl and pour the liqueur syrup over the top. Leave to marinate for at least 2 hours.

3 Peel and slice the bananas, then thread the banana and soaked fruit on to eight skewers, reserving any marinade. Cook under a hot grill for 5 minutes, turning and basting with the marinade. Serve hot.

PEACHES IN ORANGE AND VANILLA SYRUP

SERVES 4

2 oranges
115 g (4 oz) sugar
1 vanilla pod
400 ml (14 fl oz) water
6 small peaches, halved and stoned
Almond Cookies (see page 78), to serve

1 Pare the rind from one of the oranges using a zester (or use a vegetable peeler to cut wide strips and cut these into fine shreds with a sharp knife). Set aside.

2 Squeeze the juice from both oranges into a saucepan, add the sugar, vanilla pod and water and heat gently, stirring occasionally until the sugar dissolves.

3 Bring the syrup to the boil, add the peach halves and orange rind and simmer gently for 5-8 minutes until the peaches are just tender.

4 Leave to cool in the syrup, then remove the vanilla pod and serve cold with Almond Cookies.

STRAWBERRIES WITH SHERRY

SERVES 4

675 g (1½ lb) strawberries, halved
5 × 15 ml tbs cream sherry
3 × 15 ml tbs caster sugar
sprigs of fresh mint, to decorate
lightly whipped cream, to serve

1 Press 175 g (6 oz) strawberries through a fine nylon sieve, or blend in a food processor. Place in a bowl with the remaining strawberries, sherry and sugar and toss gently together.

2 Cover and leave to stand at room temperature for 45 minutes, stirring very gently once or twice. Decorate with fresh mint sprigs and serve at room temperature with a bowl of lightly whipped cream.

TOP Strawberries with Sherry
BOTTOM Peaches in Orange and Vanilla Syrup

APPLE AND ALMOND BAKE

SERVES 6

175 g (6 oz) butter
1.1 kg (2 lb) crisp eating apples, cored and cut into thick wedges
150 g (5 oz) caster sugar
finely grated rind and juice of 1 lemon
175 g (6 oz) ground almonds
3 eggs
single cream, to serve

1 Melt 50 g (2 oz) of the butter in a large frying pan until foaming. Add the apples, scatter 25 g (1 oz) of the sugar on top and cook briskly for about 5 minutes, turning the apple wedges once or twice until softened and beginning to brown.

2 Meanwhile, place all but 1 × 15 ml tbs of the remaining sugar in a mixing bowl. Add the remaining butter and beat until light and fluffy, then beat in the lemon rind and juice, almonds and eggs.

3 Transfer the apples to a well-buttered baking dish, then pour the almond mixture over. Tap the dish on the work surface once or twice to settle the mixture.

4 Bake in the oven at 200°C/400°F/Gas Mark 6 for 20-25 minutes, until the topping is set and golden brown. Sprinkle the dessert with the reserved sugar and serve warm with single cream.

WALNUT AND HONEY CAKE

SERVES 6–8

115 g (4 oz) butter
115 g (4 oz) caster sugar
3 eggs, beaten
115 g (4 oz) self-raising wholemeal flour
1 × 5 ml tsp baking powder
4 × 15 ml tbs clear honey
finely grated rind and juice of 1 lemon
175 g (6 oz) walnuts, coarsely chopped

1 Beat together the butter and sugar until very light and fluffy. Beat in the eggs a little at a time, beating well after each addition. Mix together the flour and baking powder and fold into the creamed mixture.

2 Stir in the honey, lemon rind and juice, and all but 2 × 15 ml tbs of the walnuts. Spoon into a greased and lined 1 kg (2 lb) loaf tin and spread evenly.

3 Bake in the oven at 180°C/350°F/Gas Mark 4 for about 30-40 minutes. Scatter the reserved walnuts over the surface and cook for a further 30-40 minutes or until well risen and firm to the touch.

4 Leave to cool in the tin for 10 minutes before turning out. Remove the lining paper and cool on a wire rack.

COOK'S TIP

Cover the surface of the cake with kitchen foil after 1 hour, if necessary, to prevent it over-browning.

Walnut and Honey Cake

CHOCOLATE AND NOUGAT ICE CREAM

SERVES 4–6

115 g (4 oz) milk or dark Toblerone chocolate
50 g (2 oz) plain chocolate
400 g carton fresh custard sauce
150 ml (5 fl oz) double cream
1 × 15 ml tbs clear honey
1 × 15 ml tbs sweet sherry

1 Break up the Toblerone and plain chocolate and place in a heatproof bowl set over a pan of simmering water to melt.

2 Stir the melted chocolate into the custard until thoroughly combined. Whip the cream to the same consistency as the custard and fold into the mixture. Stir in the honey and sherry.

3 Pour the mixture into a shallow freezerproof container and freeze for about 1 hour, or until the mixture has frozen 2.5 cm (1 in) from the sides.

4 Transfer the mixture to a mixing bowl and beat until smooth. Return to the container and freeze until firm.

5 Soften the ice cream in the refrigerator for about 20 minutes to serve in scoops.

RAISIN AND SHERRY ICE CREAM

SERVES 6

150 g (5 oz) raisins
300 ml (10 fl oz) cream sherry
50 g (2 oz) caster sugar
2 × 400 g cartons fresh custard sauce
300 ml (10 fl oz) double cream

1 Place the raisins in a bowl with 175 ml (6 fl oz) of the sherry and leave to soak for 2 hours.

2 Mix the sugar into the custard sauce, then stir in the raisin and sherry mixture.

3 Whip the cream until it forms soft peaks then fold into the custard mixture. Transfer to a freezerproof container and freeze for 2-3 hours until frozen around the sides. Beat thoroughly with a whisk or wooden spoon, then return to the freezer until solid.

4 Soften the ice cream in the refrigerator for about 20 minutes before serving in scoops with a little of the remaining sherry drizzled over each portion.

TORRIJAS

SERVES 4

1 small day-old French stick
225 ml (8 fl oz) milk
3 × 15 ml tbs sugar
1 cinnamon stick
rind of ½ lemon
vegetable oil, for frying
2 eggs, lightly beaten
sugar and ground cinnamon, for dusting

1 Cut the bread into eight 2 cm (¾ in) thick slices. Place in a single layer in a deep dish.

2 Put the milk, sugar, cinnamon and lemon rind in a pan. Bring to the boil and simmer for 10 minutes. Strain and pour over the bread. Leave for 2 minutes then transfer to a clean dish. Leave for 2 hours to dry.

3 Heat about 1 cm (½ in) of oil in a frying pan. Dip the bread in beaten egg and fry, turning once, until golden. Drain on absorbent kitchen paper.

4 Dredge the warm bread slices in the sugar and sprinkle with cinnamon. Serve immediately.

TOP Chocolate and Nougat Ice Cream
BOTTOM Raisin and Sherry Ice Cream

CHURROS

MAKES ABOUT 24

225 g (8 oz) plain flour

1 × 15 ml tbs vegetable oil

600 ml (1 pt) water

pinch of salt

vegetable oil, for frying

caster sugar for serving

1 Sift the flour on to a piece of greaseproof paper. Place the oil in a medium saucepan with the water and a large pinch of salt. Bring slowly to the boil. Immediately tip in all the flour and beat over a gentle heat until a smooth shiny ball forms. The mixture should be the consistency of very thick batter. Leave to cool for about 10 minutes.

2 Line two baking trays with non-stick baking parchment. Spoon the mixture into a piping bag fitted with a 1 cm (½ in) star nozzle. Pipe on to the baking trays into 8 cm (3 in) lengths or small loops. The mixture will be quite stiff to pipe – if the bag is too hot to hold, wear rubber gloves while piping the mixture.

3 Pour the vegetable oil into a frying pan to a depth of about 1 cm (½ in) and heat until very hot. Reduce the heat, then fry the churros a few at a time until barely coloured, turning once. Drain on absorbent kitchen paper. Keep warm, uncovered, in a low oven while frying the remaining churros.

4 Serve warm, sprinkled liberally with caster sugar.

COOK'S TIP

Serve these delicious fritters for a weekend breakfast treat – they are often dipped in coffee or hot chocolate before eating.

ALMOND COOKIES

MAKES 20

150 g (5 oz) plain flour

50 g (2 oz) ground almonds

90 g (3½ oz) sugar

pinch of salt

¼ × 5 ml tsp cinnamon

115 g (4 oz) margarine

1 egg, lightly beaten

icing sugar, for dusting

1 Put the flour in a heavy-based pan and cook, stirring, for about 6 minutes. Do not let the flour brown. Leave to cool.

2 Mix the almonds, sugar, salt and cinnamon with the cooled flour. Rub in the margarine and enough of the beaten egg to form a fairly stiff dough.

3 Roll the dough into 2.5 cm (1 in) balls and place on a baking tray. Flatten the centres slightly.

4 Bake at 150°C/300°F/Gas Mark 2 for about 30 minutes until golden. Leave to cool, then dust heavily with icing sugar.

TOP Almond Cookies
BOTTOM Churros

INDEX

almond: almond cookies, 78
  apple and almond bake, 74
  Santiago almond tarts, 68
apple: apple and almond bake, 74
  apple tart, 70
artichokes with potatoes and thyme,
  60
asparagus and orange salad, 64
Asturian pork and bean casserole, 40
aubergine: fried aubergine strips, 58

bacalao vegetable casserole, 48
baked ham tortilla, 30
baked tomato salad with baby spinach
  leaves, 59
beans: Asturian pork and bean casserole, 40
  garbanzo stew, 56
beef: beef with hazelnuts and pears, 42
  spicy meat turnovers, 18
biscuits: almond cookies, 78
broad beans: lamb with garlic and
  beans, 40

cake: walnut and honey cake, 75
carrots: spiced carrots, 20
Catalan tart, 68
Catalonian chicken, 34
chicken: Catalonian chicken, 34
  chicken with almonds and saffron, 36
  fiesta chicken, 34
  kidney and chicken kebabs, 17
  Spanish chicken with rice, 36
chocolate: chocolate and nougat ice
  cream, 76
  nutty fig and chocolate slice, 70
churros, 78
country-style rabbit casserole, 44
courgettes: marinated courgettes, 64

duck: Seville roast duck, 38

eggs: baked ham tortilla, 30
  eggs flamenco, 26
  mushroom revuelto, 28
  Spanish tortilla, 26
  spiced egg salad, 64
  spinach pancakes, 28
  tuna stuffed eggs, 30

fiesta chicken, 34
fig: nutty fig and chocolate slice, 70
  pork loin stuffed with figs, 39
fish: bacalao vegetable casserole, 48
  fish and leek soup, 12
  grilled sardines with fresh tomato
  sauce, 16
  haddock and prawn paella, 48
  onion and anchovy pizza, 20
  salt cod balls, 14

spinach and tuna empanada, 52
  whiting and cockles in salsa verde, 52
fried aubergine strips, 58

garbanzo stew, 56
gazpacho, 12
grilled fruit kebabs, 72
grilled prawns with romesco sauce, 50
grilled sardines with fresh tomato
  sauce, 16

haddock and prawn paella, 48

ice cream: chocolate and nougat ice
  cream, 76
  raisin and sherry ice cream, 76

kebabs: grilled fruit kebabs, 72
  kidney and chicken kebabs, 17
kidney: kidney and chicken kebabs, 17
  kidneys in sherry sauce, 42

lamb with garlic and beans, 40
leek: fish and leek soup, 12

marinated courgettes, 64
mushroom revuelto, 28
mushroom tartlets, 22

nutty fig and chocolate slice, 70

onion and anchovy pizza, 20
orange: asparagus and orange salad, 64
  grilled fruit kebabs, 72
  peaches in orange vanilla syrup, 72
  tarragon orange veal, 44

paella: haddock and prawn paella, 48
  vegetarian paella, 62
pancakes: spinach pancakes, 28
peaches in orange and vanilla syrup,
  72
peppers: stuffed peppers, 56
pizza: onion and anchovy pizza, 20
pork: Asturian pork and bean casserole,
  40
  pork and ham flamenquines, 18
  pork loin stuffed with figs, 39
potatoes: artichokes with potatoes and
  thyme, 60
  potato and rosemary cake, 60
  Spanish tortilla, 26
  spicy potatoes, 58
  wrinkled potatoes with garlic and
  paprika sauce, 22
prawn: grilled prawns with romesco
  sauce, 50
  haddock and prawn paella, 48
  prawns with garlic and oil, 14
  Spanish prawn fritters, 14

rabbit: country-style rabbit casserole,
  44
raisin and sherry ice cream, 76
rice: haddock and prawn paella, 48
  saffron and olive rice, 62
  Spanish chicken with rice, 36
  vegetarian paella, 62

saffron and olive rice, 62
salads: asparagus and orange salad, 64
  baked tomato salad with baby
  spinach leaves, 59
  spiced egg salad, 64
salt cod: bacalao vegetable casserole,
  48
  salt and cod balls, 14
Santiago almond tarts, 68
sardines: grilled sardines with fresh
  tomato sauce, 16
scallops in tomato wine sauce, 51
Seville roast duck, 38
soups: fish and leek soup, 12
  gazpacho, 12
Spanish chicken with rice, 36
Spanish prawn fritters, 14
Spanish tortilla, 26
spiced carrots, 20
spiced egg salad, 64
spicy meat turnovers, 18
spicy potatoes, 58
spinach pancakes, 28
spinach and tuna empanada, 52
strawberries with sherry, 72
stuffed peppers, 56

tarragon orange veal, 44
tart: apple tart, 70
  Catalan tart, 68
  mushroom tartlets, 22
  Santiago almond tarts, 68
torrijas, 76
tortilla: baked ham tortilla, 30
  Spanish tortilla, 26
tuna: spinach and tuna empanada, 52
  tuna stuffed eggs, 30

veal: tarragon orange veal, 44
vegetarian paella, 62

walnut and honey cake, 75
whiting and cockles in salsa verde, 52
wrinkled potatoes with garlic and
  paprika sauce, 22